No Money, No Problem:
Creative Financing Secrets

For permission requests, write to the publisher at the following address:

Pro Real Estate Books Inc.
167 Belle Terre Blvd
Covington, LA, 70433
Email: info@prorealestatebooks.com
Website: www.prorealestatebooks.com

This book is a work of fiction. Names, characters, places, and incidents either are products of the author's imagination or are used fictitiously. Any resemblance to actual events or locales or persons, living or dead, is entirely coincidental.

ISBN: 9798877364332

Printed in the United States of America

Cover design by Jane Dseroio

Interior layout and design by Jim Schiro

Visit our website at www.prorealestatebooks.com

First Printing: January 2024

TABLE OF CONTENTS

Chapter 1

Understanding Seller Financing - An Introduction

Real estate transactions can be complex and often involve various financing options. One option that both buyers and sellers may consider is seller financing. In this chapter, we will provide an introduction to the concept of seller financing, explaining what it is, how it works, and why it can be a valuable tool in real estate transactions.

What is Seller Financing?

Seller financing, also known as owner financing or seller carryback financing, is a unique arrangement in real estate transactions where the seller of a property acts as the lender. Instead of the buyer obtaining a traditional mortgage loan from a bank or a lending institution, the seller extends credit to the buyer to facilitate the purchase of the property.

In a typical seller financing arrangement, the buyer pays a down payment to the seller and agrees to make regular payments, including interest, directly to the seller over an agreed-upon period. Essentially, the seller becomes the lender, and the buyer becomes the borrower. The terms and conditions of the financing are negotiated between the buyer and the seller, allowing for flexibility and customization based on their needs and preferences.

How Does Seller Financing Work?

To better understand how seller financing works, let's break down the key components of this arrangement:

1. Negotiating the Purchase Price

In a seller financing transaction, the buyer and seller must first agree on the purchase price of the property. This price is often determined through negotiations, just like in a traditional real estate deal. The negotiated purchase price will form the basis for the seller-financed agreement.

2. Down Payment

Once the purchase price is established, the buyer typically pays a down payment to the seller. The down payment amount can vary but is usually lower than what is required by traditional mortgage lenders. This makes seller financing an attractive option for buyers who may not have access to a substantial down payment.

3. Terms and Interest Rate

The buyer and seller must also agree on the terms of the seller financing arrangement. This includes specifying the interest rate, repayment schedule, and the duration of the loan. Terms can vary widely and can be tailored to suit the needs of both parties.

4. Promissory Note and Mortgage or Deed of Trust

To formalize the seller financing agreement, the buyer and seller will typically execute a promissory note, which outlines the terms of the loan, including the interest rate, repayment schedule, and consequences of default.

Additionally, the seller may also require the buyer to sign a mortgage or deed of trust, which serves as collateral for the loan. This document gives the seller a legal claim to the property in case the buyer defaults on the loan.

5. Closing the Transaction

Once all the terms are agreed upon, the seller financing transaction can proceed to closing, just like a traditional real estate closing. At closing, all necessary documents are signed, and the buyer takes possession of the property. The seller may retain legal title to the property until the loan is fully paid off.

Why Choose Seller Financing?

Seller financing can be a beneficial option for both buyers and sellers in certain situations. Let's explore some of the advantages of choosing seller financing:

For Buyers:

1. **Flexible Qualification Requirements:** Seller financing may be more accessible to buyers with less-than-perfect credit or those who may not meet the stringent requirements of traditional lenders.

2. **Lower Down Payment:** Buyers can often secure a property with a lower down payment compared to traditional mortgages, making homeownership more achievable.

3. **Customizable Terms:** Buyers and sellers have the freedom to negotiate terms that work best for both

parties, allowing for flexibility in the repayment schedule and interest rates.

For Sellers:

1. **Attractive Selling Option:** Seller financing can make a property more appealing to potential buyers, potentially leading to a quicker sale.

2. **Steady Income Stream:** Sellers can receive a consistent stream of income through monthly payments from the buyer, which can be especially advantageous for retirees.

3. **Potential for Higher Sale Price:** By offering seller financing, sellers may be able to command a higher sale price and potentially earn more interest over the life of the loan.

4. **Tax Benefits:** Depending on the seller's circumstances, there may be potential tax advantages to receiving payments over time rather than a lump sum.

Common Misconceptions About Seller Financing

While seller financing can offer several benefits, there are also common misconceptions that need to be addressed:

1. Risk of Default: Sellers may worry about the risk of the buyer defaulting on the loan. However, proper due diligence, including credit checks and financial verification, can help mitigate this risk.

2. Limited Pool of Buyers: Some sellers believe that offering seller financing limits the pool of potential buyers. While it may attract a specific type of buyer, it can also make the property more appealing to those who might not qualify for traditional financing.

3. Difficulty in Qualification: Sellers may mistakenly think that qualifying buyers for seller financing is complex. While it does require some evaluation, it can be more flexible than traditional lending standards.

Conclusion

Seller financing is a valuable tool in the real estate industry that allows buyers and sellers to create customized financing arrangements that suit their individual needs. In this chapter, we've provided an introduction to the concept of seller financing, explained how it works, and highlighted its advantages for both buyers and sellers.

In the following chapters of this book, we will delve deeper into the intricacies of seller financing, exploring topics such as qualifying for seller financing, negotiating terms, and successfully closing seller financing transactions. By the end of this book, you'll have a comprehensive understanding of how seller financing can be a valuable strategy in the world of real estate.

In the next chapter, we will explore the benefits and drawbacks of seller financing in more detail, helping you weigh the pros and cons to determine if it's the right option for your real estate needs.

Chapter 2

Benefits and Drawbacks of Seller Financing

Seller financing offers unique advantages and disadvantages for both buyers and sellers in the real estate market. In this chapter, we will explore the benefits and drawbacks of seller financing, helping you understand whether this financing option aligns with your real estate goals and circumstances.

Benefits of Seller Financing

1. Access to Homeownership for Buyers

One of the most significant benefits of seller financing is that it can provide access to homeownership for buyers who might otherwise struggle to obtain traditional mortgage loans. Here's how seller financing benefits buyers:

Lower Down Payment Requirements

Traditional lenders often require substantial down payments, which can be a barrier for many prospective homebuyers. Seller financing allows buyers to negotiate a lower down payment, making homeownership more attainable.

Flexible Credit Requirements

Buyers with less-than-perfect credit may find it challenging to qualify for conventional mortgages. Seller financing can be more flexible in terms of credit requirements, giving those with less-than-ideal credit histories a chance to own a home.

Opportunity for Self-Employed Individuals

Self-employed individuals may have difficulty proving their income through traditional means, making it challenging to secure a mortgage. Seller financing allows for more creative income verification methods, potentially benefiting self-employed buyers.

2. Customizable Terms for Buyers and Sellers

Seller financing offers a high degree of flexibility, allowing both buyers and sellers to tailor the terms of the financing agreement to their specific needs and preferences. Here's how this flexibility benefits both parties:

Negotiable Interest Rates

Buyers and sellers can negotiate the interest rate on the seller-financed loan, potentially leading to more favorable terms compared to prevailing market rates.

Flexible Repayment Schedules

The repayment schedule, including the duration of the loan and the frequency of payments, can be customized to align with the financial situation and goals of both parties.

Unique Terms

Buyers and sellers can include unique provisions in their seller financing agreement, such as balloon payments, interest-only periods, or other terms that suit their circumstances.

3. Potential for Higher Sale Price for Sellers

Sellers can benefit financially from seller financing in several ways, including the potential for a higher sale price:

Attracting More Buyers

By offering seller financing, sellers can make their property more attractive to potential buyers who may not qualify for traditional mortgages. This increased demand can lead to a higher sale price.

Interest Income

Sellers receive interest income on the loan provided to the buyer. Over time, this interest income can significantly boost the seller's overall return on the property.

Flexibility in Sale Price

Sellers can often command a higher sale price when offering seller financing, as they have the flexibility to negotiate terms that appeal to the buyer.

4. Steady Income Stream for Sellers

Seller financing provides sellers with a steady stream of income, which can be particularly advantageous in certain situations:

Consistent Cash Flow

Sellers receive regular monthly payments from the buyer, creating a predictable cash flow stream that can be useful for budgeting and financial planning.

Retirement Income

Seller financing can serve as a source of income for sellers who have retired or are looking for a reliable income stream during retirement.

Tax Benefits

Depending on the seller's tax situation, there may be potential tax benefits associated with receiving payments over time rather than as a lump sum.

Drawbacks of Seller Financing

While seller financing offers many advantages, it is essential to consider the potential drawbacks and risks associated with this financing option.

1. Risk of Default

One of the primary concerns for sellers in seller financing transactions is the risk of the buyer defaulting on the loan. If the buyer stops making payments, the seller may need to go through the foreclosure process to regain possession of the property. This can be time-consuming and costly.

Mitigating the Risk

Sellers can mitigate the risk of default by conducting thorough due diligence on the buyer's financial situation, including credit checks and income verification. Additionally, including a well-drafted promissory note and mortgage or deed of trust can provide legal recourse in case of default.

2. Limited Pool of Buyers

Offering seller financing can limit the pool of potential buyers, as it may only attract those who specifically seek this type of financing. Some sellers may be concerned that they won't find a buyer willing to accept seller financing terms.

Balancing Act

Sellers must strike a balance between attracting potential buyers and ensuring that the terms of the financing arrangement are reasonable and favorable for both parties. Marketing the property effectively can help find suitable buyers.

3. Difficulty in Qualification

While seller financing can offer flexibility, sellers still need to evaluate the financial qualifications of potential buyers to minimize the risk of default. This evaluation process can be complex and time-consuming.

Seeking Professional Assistance

Sellers may benefit from seeking the assistance of real estate professionals or legal experts to navigate the qualification process effectively.

4. Delayed Access to Full Sale Proceeds

Sellers who opt for seller financing will not receive the full sale proceeds upfront. Instead, they will receive payments over the agreed-upon duration of the loan, which could be several years.

Planning and Budgeting

Sellers should carefully plan and budget for their financial needs, considering that the full sale proceeds will be received gradually.

Conclusion

Seller financing offers a unique and flexible financing option in the real estate market. Buyers can benefit from lower down payments, flexible credit requirements, and customizable terms, while sellers can attract more buyers, earn interest

income, and enjoy a steady income stream. However, it's essential to be aware of the potential drawbacks, such as the risk of default and the need to evaluate buyer qualifications.

In the next chapter, we will delve into the nitty-gritty details of how to qualify for seller financing as a buyer, including steps to take to enhance your eligibility and increase your chances of securing seller financing for your dream property. Understanding the qualification process is crucial for both buyers and sellers considering this financing option.

Chapter 3

The Basics of Real Estate Transactions

In the world of real estate, understanding the fundamentals of property transactions is crucial, whether you're a buyer or a seller. This chapter explores the essential aspects of real estate transactions, providing valuable insights into the processes involved and the key players in the game.

The Real Estate Transaction Process

Real estate transactions involve a series of well-defined steps, each playing a pivotal role in the buying and selling process. Let's take a closer look at these stages:

1. Property Search and Selection: Buyers begin by defining their property criteria, including location, size, budget, and specific features. They collaborate with a real estate agent to identify suitable properties, visit them, and assess whether they meet their needs.

Sellers, on the other hand, prepare their property for sale, ensuring it's clean and well-maintained. They work closely with a real estate agent to effectively market the property.

2. Negotiation and Offer: Once a suitable property is found, buyers make an offer that includes the purchase price, contingencies, and financing terms. Negotiations take place between the buyer and seller until mutually acceptable terms and a final price are agreed upon.

3. Contract and Due Diligence: Buyers, with the assistance of a real estate attorney or agent, draft a purchase contract once an agreement is reached. They also conduct due diligence, which may involve property inspections, title searches, and financial evaluations.

Sellers cooperate with the buyer's due diligence process, providing access to the property and relevant documents. They address any concerns or issues that arise during this phase.

4. Financing and Mortgage Approval: Buyers secure financing for the property, either through traditional mortgage lenders or seller financing. They complete the mortgage application and provide the necessary documentation.

In the case of seller financing, sellers work with the buyer to finalize the financing agreement and complete the required paperwork.

5. Closing Preparations: Buyers coordinate with the lender and the seller to ensure that all required documentation is in order for the closing.

Sellers work alongside the buyer to facilitate the closing process, providing any necessary documentation and signatures.

6. Closing: The closing meeting is where all the pieces come together. Buyers attend this meeting, where they sign all necessary documents, and funds are transferred.

Sellers also attend the closing meeting and sign documents to transfer ownership to the buyer.

7. Post-Closing: After closing, buyers take possession of the property and begin homeownership. They continue to make mortgage payments or seller financing payments as agreed upon.

Sellers ensure that the property title is transferred to the buyer and that all obligations under the financing agreement are met.

Key Players in Real Estate Transactions

Successful real estate transactions require collaboration among various professionals and individuals, each with their own specialized roles. Let's explore who these key players are:

1. Real Estate Agents: Real estate agents, often referred to as Realtors, represent buyers and sellers in real estate transactions. They assist in property search, negotiations, and guiding clients through the entire process.

- Buyer's Agent: Helps buyers find suitable properties, advises on market conditions, negotiates on behalf of the buyer, and assists with due diligence and closing.

- Seller's Agent: Represents the seller in marketing and selling the property, assists with pricing strategies, negotiates offers from potential buyers, and coordinates the transaction process.

2. Real Estate Attorneys: Real estate attorneys ensure that transactions are legally sound and protect their clients' interests. They are often involved in contract drafting and review, title searches, and the closing process.

- Buyer's Attorney: Reviews the purchase contract, conducts title searches, and ensures all legal requirements are met for a smooth closing.

- Seller's Attorney: Reviews offers and purchase contracts on behalf of the seller, assists in addressing legal concerns or disputes, and ensures the seller's legal obligations are fulfilled.

3. Mortgage Lenders: Mortgage lenders provide financing to buyers to facilitate property purchases. Buyers can choose from various lenders, including banks, credit unions, and mortgage brokers.

- Traditional Mortgage Lenders: Evaluate the buyer's creditworthiness, offer mortgage options with different terms and interest rates, and process mortgage applications for approval.

4. Home Inspectors: Home inspectors assess the property's condition to identify any existing or potential issues. Their findings influence negotiations and impact the buyer's decision to proceed with the purchase.

- Buyer's Home Inspector: Conducts a thorough property inspection, provides a detailed report on issues or needed repairs, and helps the buyer make informed decisions.

5. Title Companies and Title Agents: Title companies and their agents conduct title searches, ensure property title clarity, and facilitate ownership transfers.

- Buyer's Title Agent: Conducts title searches, issues title insurance policies to protect the buyer, and verifies ownership history.

- **Seller's Title Agent:** Facilitates the title transfer process and provides necessary documentation to clear title issues.

6. Appraisers: Appraisers determine the property's fair market value to ensure that the purchase price aligns with its worth, helping lenders decide how much they are willing to finance.

- **Buyer's Appraiser:** Evaluates the property's condition and market value, providing an appraisal report for mortgage approval purposes.

7. Escrow Officers: Escrow officers or companies serve as neutral third parties in real estate transactions, holding funds and essential documents in escrow until all sale conditions are met.

- **Roles of Escrow Officers:** Safeguard the buyer's earnest money deposit, ensure that all required documents are signed, and funds are distributed correctly at closing.

Legal and Regulatory Considerations

Real estate transactions are subject to various legal and regulatory requirements that vary by location. It's crucial for both buyers and sellers to be aware of these considerations, which may include local zoning laws, property disclosure requirements, environmental regulations, and tax implications.

Seeking legal advice and working with experienced professionals can help navigate the legal and regulatory complexities associated with real estate transactions.

Conclusion

Understanding the basics of real estate transactions, from the initial property search to the closing process, is essential for anyone involved in buying or selling real estate. In the next chapter, we will explore the various ways buyers can secure financing for their real estate purchases, including a detailed look at seller financing as a viable option for those seeking flexibility and customization in their financing arrangements.

Chapter 4

Financing Your Real Estate Purchase

In the previous chapters, we've explored the intricacies of seller financing and the essential steps in a real estate transaction. Now, it's time to delve deeper into the various financing options available to buyers, with a specific focus on seller financing. Whether you're a buyer looking for flexibility or a seller considering this financing method, this chapter will provide you with valuable insights into the world of real estate financing.

Traditional Mortgage Financing

Before we delve into seller financing, let's start with the most common form of real estate financing—traditional mortgage loans. These loans are provided by banks, credit unions, mortgage lenders, and government agencies like the Federal Housing Administration (FHA) or the Department of Veterans Affairs (VA). Here's an overview of traditional mortgage financing:

1. Mortgage Application and Approval

The process begins with the buyer applying for a mortgage loan. This typically involves submitting financial documents, such as income statements, tax returns, and credit reports, to the lender. The lender evaluates the buyer's creditworthiness, income, and debt-to-income ratio to determine eligibility.

2. Down Payment

Buyers are usually required to make a down payment as part of the mortgage financing process. The down payment amount can vary but is often around 20% of the property's purchase price. However, some mortgage programs offer lower down payment options, such as 3.5% for FHA loans.

3. Interest Rates and Terms

Once approved, buyers receive a mortgage loan with specific terms, including an interest rate and repayment period. The interest rate can be fixed (stays the same throughout the loan term) or adjustable (varies based on market conditions).

4. Monthly Mortgage Payments

Buyers are responsible for making monthly mortgage payments, which include both principal and interest. These payments continue over the agreed-upon loan term, which can vary but is often 15, 20, or 30 years.

5. Property Appraisal

The lender typically requires a property appraisal to ensure that the property's value aligns with the loan amount. The appraiser assesses the property's condition and recent sales of comparable properties in the area.

6. Private Mortgage Insurance (PMI)

If the buyer's down payment is less than 20% of the purchase price, they may be required to pay for private mortgage insurance (PMI). PMI protects the lender in case the borrower defaults on the loan.

7. Closing Costs

Buyers should budget for closing costs, which include fees for services like title searches, inspections, and legal expenses. These costs are typically paid at the closing of the transaction.

Traditional mortgage financing offers buyers a well-established and regulated path to homeownership. However, it may not be the best fit for everyone, especially those looking for alternative financing options with more flexibility.

Seller Financing: A Closer Look

Seller financing, also known as owner financing or seller carryback financing, is an alternative method for buyers to acquire a property. In seller financing, the seller becomes the lender, offering a loan to the buyer to facilitate the purchase. Let's explore the key aspects of seller financing:

1. Negotiating Terms

Seller financing allows for flexibility in negotiating the terms of the financing agreement. Buyers and sellers can discuss and agree upon various aspects of the loan, including:

- **Interest Rate:** Buyers and sellers can negotiate the interest rate, which may be higher or lower than prevailing market rates, depending on the terms of the agreement.

- **Down Payment:** Sellers can often accept a lower down payment than what traditional lenders require, making it more accessible for buyers.

- **Repayment Schedule:** The repayment schedule, including the duration of the loan and the frequency of payments, can be customized to align with both parties' financial situations.

2. Qualifying for Seller Financing

Qualifying for seller financing can be more straightforward than traditional mortgage financing in some cases. Sellers have the flexibility to consider factors beyond just the buyer's credit score, such as the buyer's financial stability, employment history, and even their personal relationship with the buyer.

3. Balloon Payments

One unique feature of seller financing is the potential for a balloon payment. A balloon payment is a large, lump-sum payment that becomes due at the end of the loan term. This can be advantageous for buyers who expect a significant financial event, such as an inheritance or bonus, in the future.

4. Legal Protections

To protect both parties, seller financing typically involves the creation of legal documents, including a promissory note and a mortgage or deed of trust. These documents outline the terms of the loan, the consequences of default, and the process for addressing any disputes.

5. Risks and Considerations

While seller financing offers unique advantages, it's essential to be aware of the potential risks:

- **Risk of Default:** If the buyer defaults on the loan, the seller may need to go through the foreclosure process to regain possession of the property, which can be time-consuming and costly.

- **Limited Pool of Buyers:** Offering seller financing can limit the pool of potential buyers, as it may only attract those specifically seeking this type of financing.

- **Difficulty in Qualification:** Sellers must evaluate the financial qualifications of potential buyers to minimize the risk of default, which can be complex and time-consuming.

- **Delayed Access to Full Sale Proceeds:** Sellers will not receive the full sale proceeds upfront but rather over the agreed-upon duration of the loan, which could be several years.

Is Seller Financing Right for You?

Whether you are a buyer or a seller, the decision to use seller financing should be based on your individual circumstances and financial goals. Here are some factors to consider:

For Buyers:

- **Financial Situation:** Do you have a stable income and the ability to make regular payments?

- **Credit History:** Is your credit history less than perfect, making it challenging to qualify for a traditional mortgage?

- **Flexibility:** Are you seeking a financing option with flexible terms, including a lower down payment?

- **Long-Term Plans:** Do you plan to stay in the property for an extended period, or are you prepared for potential changes in the loan terms, such as a balloon payment?

For Sellers:

- **Market Conditions:** Is the real estate market in your area conducive to offering seller financing, with a potential for attracting more buyers?

- **Financial Goals:** Are you looking for a steady income stream, potentially earning interest income on the loan provided to the buyer?

- **Risk Tolerance:** Are you comfortable with the potential risk of default and the need to go through the foreclosure process if the buyer fails to make payments?

- **Property Sale Price:** Do you believe that offering seller financing can command a higher sale price for your property?

Conclusion

Financing a real estate purchase is a critical aspect of the homebuying process. Traditional mortgage financing provides a well-established route to homeownership, while seller financing offers flexibility and customization in the financing arrangement. Understanding the key features of both options can help buyers and sellers make informed decisions that align with their unique goals and circumstances.

In the next chapter, we will explore the practical steps involved in securing seller financing, from finding a willing seller to negotiating favorable terms and completing the necessary documentation

Chapter 5

Securing Seller Financing

In the previous chapters, we've discussed the fundamentals of real estate transactions and explored the intricacies of seller financing. Now, it's time to delve into the practical steps involved in securing seller financing. Whether you're a buyer seeking this financing option or a seller considering offering it, understanding the process is essential to navigate the complexities of seller financing successfully.

Step 1: Identify Potential Sellers

The first step in securing seller financing is to identify potential sellers who may be willing to consider this financing option. Here are some strategies to help you find suitable sellers:

Explore Off-Market Properties: Look for properties that are not listed on the open market. These may include properties owned by individuals who are not actively trying to sell but might be open to the idea of seller financing.

Network within Your Community: Attend local real estate events, join real estate investor groups, and connect with real estate agents and professionals in your community. Word of mouth can lead you to sellers interested in creative financing options.

Target Distressed Properties: Properties facing financial difficulties or in need of repairs may present opportunities for seller financing. Approach owners facing foreclosure or properties with a history of extended time on the market.

Explore Niche Markets: Certain niche markets, such as retirement communities or vacation properties, may have sellers more open to seller financing due to the specific demographics and motivations of the sellers.

Step 2: Approach Potential Sellers

Once you've identified potential sellers, the next step is to approach them with your proposal for seller financing. Here's how to do it effectively:

Build Rapport: Establish a rapport with the seller by demonstrating your genuine interest in their property. Be courteous and professional in your approach.

Present Your Offer: Clearly present your offer for seller financing. Explain the benefits, such as the potential for a higher sale price, steady income from interest, and a broader pool of potential buyers.

Negotiate Terms: Be prepared to negotiate terms, including the interest rate, down payment, loan duration, and any other relevant details. Flexibility and a willingness to find mutually beneficial terms are key.

Address Concerns: Listen to the seller's concerns and address them. Common concerns may include the risk of default, ensuring a fair market interest rate, and the seller's ability to access funds from the sale.

Document the Agreement: Once both parties agree on the terms, document the agreement in writing. It's essential to have a clear and legally binding contract that outlines the financing terms and conditions.

Step 3: Conduct Due Diligence

Before finalizing the seller financing agreement, both buyers and sellers should conduct due diligence to protect their interests. Here's what each party should consider:

For Buyers:

Property Inspection: Conduct a thorough property inspection to identify any issues that may affect its value or habitability. This can be a crucial negotiation point for repairs or adjustments to the purchase price.

Title Search: Perform a title search to ensure there are no outstanding liens, encumbrances, or legal issues associated with the property's title. The title must be clear for the transaction to proceed smoothly.

Financial Review: Review your financial situation to ensure that you can meet the terms of the financing agreement comfortably. Consider factors such as your income stability and ability to make regular payments.

For Sellers:

Buyer's Creditworthiness: Evaluate the buyer's creditworthiness, financial stability, and employment history. Consider requesting financial documentation to assess the buyer's ability to meet their obligations.

Legal Protections: Consult with an attorney to draft a comprehensive seller financing agreement that outlines the terms, consequences of default, and dispute resolution processes. Legal protections are essential for both parties.

Property Value: Ensure that the property's value aligns with the agreed-upon purchase price. An appraisal may be necessary to confirm that the property's worth matches the loan amount.

Step 4: Finalize the Financing Agreement

With due diligence completed and concerns addressed, it's time to finalize the seller financing agreement. This involves several critical steps:

Draft the Legal Documents: Collaborate with an attorney to draft the necessary legal documents, including a promissory note and a mortgage or deed of trust. These documents define the terms of the loan, specify the consequences of default, and establish the legal framework for the transaction.

Sign the Agreement: Both parties should review and sign the seller financing agreement. Ensure that all terms and conditions are clear and agreed upon before signing.

Record the Mortgage: In many cases, the mortgage or deed of trust is recorded with the appropriate government authority. This serves to protect the seller's interests and establishes the lien on the property.

Arrange for Escrow: Consider using an escrow service to handle the transfer of funds and legal documents. Escrow services provide a neutral third party that ensures a smooth and secure transaction.

Step 5: Begin Loan Repayments

Once the seller financing agreement is finalized, it's time to initiate loan repayments. Here's what both parties should expect:

For Buyers:

Make Regular Payments: Adhere to the agreed-upon repayment schedule, making regular payments as outlined in the financing agreement.

Keep Records: Maintain records of all payments made, including copies of checks or electronic transaction confirmations. This documentation is essential for both parties.

Communicate: Maintain open communication with the seller throughout the loan term. Notify them promptly of any changes in your financial situation or any challenges you may face.

For Sellers:

Receive Payments: Expect to receive regular payments from the buyer as per the agreed-upon schedule.

Monitor the Loan: Keep track of the buyer's payments and ensure they are made on time. Be prepared to address any missed payments or issues promptly.

Provide Documentation: If requested by the buyer, provide documentation confirming receipt of payments, such as receipts or statements.

Step 6: Address Default and Disputes

While seller financing can be a mutually beneficial arrangement, it's essential to be prepared for the possibility of default or disputes. Here's how to address these challenges:

For Buyers:

Communicate with the Seller: If you encounter financial difficulties or anticipate missing a payment, communicate with the seller promptly. They may be willing to work out a temporary solution.

Seek Legal Advice: If you face foreclosure due to default, consult with an attorney experienced in real estate law to explore your options and potentially negotiate a resolution.

For Sellers:

Understand Legal Remedies: Familiarize yourself with the legal remedies available in case of default. These may include foreclosure, the repossession of the property, or negotiation for a modified agreement.

Consult with Legal Counsel: If a dispute arises, consult with an attorney to explore legal options and ensure that your interests are protected.

Conclusion

Securing seller financing can offer a unique and flexible path to homeownership or property sale. By identifying potential sellers, approaching them professionally, conducting due diligence, finalizing legal documents, and maintaining clear communication throughout the loan term, both buyers and sellers can navigate the seller financing process successfully.

Chapter 6

Tips for a Successful Seller Financing Transaction

Seller financing can be an excellent option for both buyers and sellers in the real estate market. It offers flexibility, a larger pool of potential buyers, and the potential for higher sale prices. However, for a seller financing transaction to be successful, it's crucial to navigate the process carefully. In this chapter, we will explore essential tips for a successful seller financing transaction, providing you with guidance on how to make this financing option work effectively for both parties involved.

1. Open and Transparent Communication

Clear and open communication between the buyer and seller is fundamental to a successful seller financing transaction. Both parties should feel comfortable discussing their expectations, concerns, and any potential issues that may arise. Here are some key communication considerations:

- **Set Expectations:** Establish clear expectations from the beginning, including the terms of the financing agreement, repayment schedule, and any special conditions.

- **Be Responsive:** Respond promptly to inquiries and requests for information. Delays in communication can lead to misunderstandings and frustration.

- **Address Concerns:** Encourage both parties to express their concerns openly and work together to find solutions. Addressing concerns early can prevent misunderstandings down the road.

- **Regular Updates:** Maintain regular updates on the progress of the transaction, including payment reminders and important milestones.

2. Seek Professional Guidance

Navigating a seller financing transaction can be complex, and it's essential to seek professional guidance to ensure that the process is handled correctly. Here are some professionals whose expertise can be invaluable:

- **Real Estate Agents:** Experienced real estate agents can assist both buyers and sellers in finding suitable financing arrangements, negotiating terms, and ensuring that the transaction complies with local laws and regulations.

- **Attorneys:** Real estate attorneys can draft the necessary legal documents, review contracts, and provide guidance on legal requirements and protections for both parties.

- **Financial Advisors:** Financial advisors can help buyers assess their financial situation and plan for successful loan repayment. Sellers may also benefit from financial advice on managing the proceeds from the sale.

- **Accountants and Tax Professionals:** Tax professionals can advise both parties on the tax implications of the transaction, including any capital gains treatment or deductions.

3. Legal Protections and Documentation

A well-drafted seller financing agreement is essential to protect the interests of both the buyer and seller. Here are some key considerations regarding legal protections and documentation:

- **Work with an Attorney:** Engage a real estate attorney to draft a comprehensive seller financing agreement that outlines all terms and conditions, including interest rates, down payments, loan duration, and consequences of default.

- **Include Contingencies:** The agreement should include contingency clauses that address potential issues, such as missed payments, property damage, or changes in financial circumstances.

- **Clear Consequences of Default:** Clearly define the consequences of default in the agreement, outlining the steps that will be taken in the event of non-payment.

- **Record the Mortgage:** In many cases, the mortgage or deed of trust should be recorded with the appropriate government authority to establish the lien on the property and protect the seller's interests.

- **Compliance with Local Laws:** Ensure that the seller financing agreement complies with local real estate laws and regulations.

4. Due Diligence

Both buyers and sellers should conduct thorough due diligence to minimize potential risks and ensure a successful transaction. Due diligence involves assessing various aspects of the property and the transaction:

For Buyers:

- **Property Inspection:** Conduct a comprehensive property inspection to identify any issues that may affect its value or habitability. This inspection can be a crucial negotiation point for repairs or adjustments to the purchase price.

- **Title Search:** Perform a title search to ensure there are no outstanding liens, encumbrances, or legal issues associated with the property's title. A clear title is essential for a smooth transaction.

- **Financial Review:** Review your financial situation carefully to ensure that you can comfortably meet the terms of the financing agreement. Consider factors such as your income stability and ability to make regular payments.

For Sellers:

- **Buyer's Financial Stability:** Evaluate the buyer's financial stability and ability to meet the terms of the financing agreement. Request financial documentation to assess the buyer's creditworthiness.

- **Property Value:** Ensure that the property's appraised value aligns with the agreed-upon purchase price. An appraisal may be necessary to confirm that the property's worth matches the loan amount.

5. Flexibility and Negotiation

Seller financing offers flexibility in terms of negotiating the terms of the agreement. Both parties should approach the negotiation process with flexibility and a willingness to find mutually beneficial terms. Here are some negotiation considerations:

- **Interest Rates:** Negotiate the interest rate, considering prevailing market rates and the financial goals of both parties. Be open to compromises that align with the current economic environment.

- **Down Payment:** Discuss the down payment amount, which can vary based on the buyer's financial situation and the seller's preferences. A lower down payment can make the property more accessible to the buyer.

- **Loan Duration:** Determine the duration of the loan and the frequency of payments. Some seller financing agreements may have shorter loan terms, while others may extend over several years.

- **Balloon Payments:** If applicable, negotiate the terms of any balloon payments, ensuring that both parties are comfortable with the lump-sum payment due at the end of the loan term.

6. Maintain Detailed Records

Throughout the seller financing transaction, it's crucial to maintain detailed records of all interactions, payments, and documentation. These records serve as a critical resource for both parties and can help resolve disputes or discrepancies. Here's what to keep track of:

- **Payment Records:** Maintain records of all payments made, including copies of checks, electronic transaction confirmations, or receipts for cash payments.

- **Communication Logs:** Document all communication between the buyer and seller, including emails, letters, and notes from phone conversations or in-person meetings.

- **Legal Documents:** Keep copies of all legal documents, including the seller financing agreement, property deeds, and any contracts related to the transaction.

- **Property Inspection Reports:** If applicable, retain the results of property inspections and any reports on repairs or renovations.

7. Plan for Contingencies

No transaction is without its potential challenges or unexpected developments. Both parties should have contingency plans in place to address these contingencies and ensure the transaction's success:

- **Missed Payments:** Plan for how missed payments will be addressed, including potential penalties, grace periods, or alternative payment arrangements.

- **Property Damage:** Consider how property damage or issues discovered after the sale will be handled, including repairs and adjustments to the purchase price.

- **Changes in Financial Circumstances:** Be prepared for changes in financial circumstances for both the buyer and seller. This may involve renegotiating terms or finding alternative solutions.

Conclusion

Seller financing can be a mutually beneficial option for buyers and sellers in the real estate market. By following these tips for a successful seller financing transaction, both parties can navigate the process with confidence and ensure a smooth and positive experience. Remember that professional guidance, open communication, and thorough due diligence are key to a successful seller financing arrangement.

In the next chapter, we will explore real-life case studies of seller financing transactions, providing practical examples of how this financing method has been employed successfully in various real estate scenarios.

Chapter 7

Real-Life Case Studies of Seller Financing Transactions

To gain a deeper understanding of how seller financing can be applied in real-world scenarios, let's explore some case studies that highlight successful seller financing transactions. These examples demonstrate the versatility of seller financing and how it can benefit both buyers and sellers in various real estate situations.

Case Study 1: The Reluctant Retiree

Background: Susan, a homeowner approaching retirement, wanted to downsize her property and generate additional income for her retirement years. She owned a spacious suburban home in a desirable neighborhood but had been struggling to attract a traditional buyer.

Challenges: Susan's property had been on the market for several months without much interest. She was reluctant to lower the sale price, as she had substantial equity in the home and wanted to maximize her return.

Solution: Susan decided to explore seller financing as an alternative. She found a young family interested in her property but unable to secure a traditional mortgage due to a recent job change that affected their creditworthiness. Susan offered to finance the sale herself, providing a win-win solution.

Outcome: The buyers agreed to a competitive interest rate, and Susan received a substantial down payment. The seller financing arrangement allowed Susan to downsize to a smaller property, generate monthly income through interest payments, and achieve a higher sale price than she initially anticipated. The buyers, despite their credit challenges, were able to purchase their dream home.

Case Study 2: The Multigenerational Investment

Background: The Garcia family, a close-knit multigenerational household, decided to invest in a rental property to generate additional income. They found a property in a desirable area, but traditional lenders were hesitant to provide financing due to the family's complex financial situation.

Challenges: The Garcia family faced difficulties securing a traditional mortgage due to varying credit scores and income sources among family members. They needed a financing solution that accommodated their unique situation.

Solution: The seller, understanding the potential of the property as a rental investment, agreed to seller financing. The family was allowed to structure the financing agreement in a way that divided ownership among family members based on their financial contributions.

Outcome: The Garcias successfully purchased the property with the seller's financing assistance. They established a clear ownership structure, with responsibilities for property management and rental income distribution. The rental property became a stable source of income for the multigenerational household, allowing them to strengthen family ties while building wealth through real estate.

Case Study 3: The Renovation Opportunity

Background: Mark, a real estate investor, identified a distressed property with significant renovation potential in an up-and-coming neighborhood. Traditional lenders were wary of financing the property due to its poor condition, and Mark needed creative financing to make the project viable.

Challenges: The property required extensive renovations, and Mark's financial resources were tied up in other real estate investments. Securing a traditional mortgage for the distressed property seemed unlikely.

Solution: Mark approached the property owner, who was eager to sell but struggled to find a buyer willing to take on the renovation project. They agreed to a seller financing arrangement that allowed Mark to purchase the property with a lower down payment, making it feasible for him to allocate resources to the necessary renovations.

Outcome: Mark successfully renovated the property, increasing its value significantly. The seller benefited from receiving a higher sale price than initially expected, and Mark, after completing the renovations, was able to secure a traditional mortgage based on the property's improved condition. The seller financing arrangement facilitated a mutually beneficial transaction that transformed a distressed property into a profitable investment.

Case Study 4: The Entrepreneurial Buyer

Background: Sarah, an aspiring entrepreneur, dreamed of starting her own business and needed a commercial property to house her venture. She found a suitable property but faced challenges securing a commercial mortgage due to her limited business history.

Challenges: Sarah's entrepreneurial spirit was hindered by the difficulty in obtaining commercial financing as a new business owner. Traditional lenders were hesitant to extend credit, which threatened her dream of establishing her business.

Solution: The property owner, impressed by Sarah's business plan and enthusiasm, agreed to seller financing for the commercial property. They structured the agreement with flexible terms that aligned with Sarah's anticipated business growth and income projections.

Outcome: Sarah was able to acquire the commercial property and launch her business successfully. The seller financing arrangement allowed her to build a track record of business success, and as her business grew, she was in a better position to secure traditional financing. The seller financing served as a stepping stone to Sarah's entrepreneurial journey.

Case Study 5: The Real Estate Portfolio Expansion

Background: John, an experienced real estate investor, had built a successful portfolio of rental properties. He identified a promising investment opportunity but needed additional capital to make the acquisition.

Challenges: John's existing real estate holdings were generating steady income, but his available liquidity was limited. He required additional funds to take advantage of the investment opportunity.

Solution: John reached out to a fellow real estate investor who owned a property with substantial equity and was interested in diversifying their investments. They agreed to a seller financing arrangement in which the investor provided financing to John for the new acquisition.

Outcome: With the assistance of seller financing, John expanded his real estate portfolio and capitalized on the investment opportunity. The seller benefited from earning interest income on the loan while still maintaining their ownership of the original property. The arrangement allowed both parties to achieve their investment goals.

Case Study 6: The Retirement Income Strategy

Background: Robert and Lisa, a retired couple, owned a rental property that generated rental income but required ongoing property management. They were considering selling the property to simplify their retirement lifestyle.

Challenges: Robert and Lisa were concerned about losing the rental income that had been an essential part of their retirement finances. They were also reluctant to sell the property at a lower price to expedite the sale.

Solution: The couple explored seller financing as an alternative to selling the property outright. They found a buyer interested in purchasing the property with a seller financing arrangement that allowed them to continue receiving monthly payments, maintaining their retirement income stream.

Outcome: Robert and Lisa retained ownership of the property while enjoying the benefits of regular income from the buyer's monthly payments. The buyer, on the other hand, gained access to the property without a large upfront payment. The seller financing arrangement provided a stable income source for the retiring couple while allowing the property to change hands gradually.

Conclusion

These real-life case studies illustrate the diverse range of situations in which seller financing can be employed successfully in real estate transactions. From helping homeowners transition into retirement to enabling entrepreneurs to start their businesses, seller financing offers flexible solutions that benefit both buyers and sellers.

As you consider the possibilities of seller financing in your own real estate endeavors, remember the importance of open communication, professional guidance, legal protections, due diligence, negotiation, and documentation. By leveraging these tips and learning from these case studies, you can navigate seller financing transactions with confidence and achieve your real estate goals.

Chapter 8

Mitigating Risks in Seller Financing

Seller financing is a versatile and beneficial financing option in real estate, but like any financial transaction, it comes with its own set of risks and challenges. Both buyers and sellers must be aware of these risks and take proactive measures to mitigate them effectively. In this chapter, we will explore the potential risks associated with seller financing and provide guidance on how to reduce and manage these risks for a successful transaction.

Understanding the Risks

Before diving into risk mitigation strategies, let's first understand the key risks associated with seller financing for both buyers and sellers.

Risks for Buyers:

1. **Default Risk:** One of the most significant risks for buyers is the potential for default. If the buyer fails to make payments as agreed, it can lead to legal complications and the potential loss of the property.

2. **Interest Rate Risk:** Buyers may face interest rate risk if the interest rate on the seller-financed loan is not fixed. Fluctuating interest rates can significantly impact the affordability of the loan.

3. **Property Condition:** Buyers risk discovering undisclosed property issues or defects after the purchase. Without proper due diligence, they may inherit costly repairs.

4. **Title Issues:** A failure to conduct a thorough title search can result in undiscovered liens or legal disputes related to the property's title.

5. **Dependence on Seller:** Buyers relying on seller financing may be overly dependent on the seller's financial stability and willingness to cooperate throughout the loan term.

Risks for Sellers:

1. **Default Risk:** Sellers face the risk of the buyer defaulting on the loan, which can lead to a lengthy and costly foreclosure process.

2. **Property Devaluation:** If the property's value decreases during the loan term, the seller may struggle to recoup their investment if the buyer defaults.

3. **Lack of Liquidity:** Sellers may find themselves lacking liquidity as they wait for the buyer to make payments over time, potentially affecting their financial plans.

4. **Legal Complexities:** Seller financing agreements can become legally complex, and sellers may face challenges if they need to enforce the terms of the agreement.

5. **Regulatory Compliance:** Sellers must ensure they comply with all relevant local and state regulations governing seller financing to avoid legal complications.

Mitigating Risks for Buyers

Buyers can take several proactive steps to mitigate the risks associated with seller financing:

1. Conduct Due Diligence:

- **Property Inspection:** Prior to purchasing, conduct a thorough property inspection to identify any hidden issues. Negotiate repairs or adjustments to the purchase price if necessary.

- **Title Search:** Ensure a comprehensive title search is performed to confirm a clear title and uncover any outstanding liens or disputes.

- **Financial Review:** Assess your financial stability and ability to make regular payments. Be realistic about your financial capacity to avoid overextending yourself.

2. Consult with Professionals:

- **Real Estate Attorney:** Consult with a real estate attorney to review the seller financing agreement and ensure it provides adequate protection for your interests.

- **Financial Advisor:** Seek advice from a financial advisor to evaluate the long-term affordability of the seller-financed loan and assess your overall financial strategy.

3. Negotiate Favorable Terms:

- **Interest Rate:** Negotiate the interest rate to ensure it aligns with your financial goals and expectations. Consider seeking a fixed interest rate for stability.

- **Down Payment:** Discuss the down payment amount with the seller, aiming for a reasonable amount that suits your financial situation.

- **Loan Duration:** Negotiate the loan duration to align with your repayment capacity and long-term plans.

- **Contingencies:** Include contingency clauses in the agreement to address potential issues like missed payments or property defects.

4. Build a Good Relationship:

- **Open Communication:** Maintain open and respectful communication with the seller throughout the loan term. Promptly inform them of any changes in your financial situation or challenges you may face.

- **Payment Records:** Keep detailed records of all payments made, including copies of checks or electronic transaction confirmations.

5. Prepare for Default Scenarios:

- **Emergency Fund:** Maintain an emergency fund to cover potential missed payments or unexpected expenses related to the property.

- **Legal Advice:** If you foresee difficulties making payments, consult with an attorney experienced in real estate law to explore your options and potentially negotiate a resolution with the seller.

Mitigating Risks for Sellers

Sellers can also take proactive measures to mitigate risks associated with seller financing:

1. Screen Buyers Carefully:

- **Creditworthiness:** Evaluate the buyer's creditworthiness, financial stability, and employment history. Request financial documentation to assess their ability to meet their obligations.

- **Background Check:** Consider conducting background checks to gain insight into the buyer's financial history and any potential red flags.

2. Legal Protections:

- **Comprehensive Agreement:** Work with a real estate attorney to draft a comprehensive seller financing agreement. Include clear terms, consequences of default, and dispute resolution processes.

- **Documentation:** Maintain detailed records of all transactions, payments, and correspondence related to the seller financing agreement.

3. Property Valuation:

- **Appraisal:** Ensure the property's appraised value aligns with the agreed-upon purchase price. An appraisal can confirm that the property's worth matches the loan amount.

- **Repairs:** Address any necessary repairs or improvements to enhance the property's value and appeal to the buyer.

4. Plan for Default and Disputes:

- **Legal Remedies:** Familiarize yourself with the legal remedies available in case of buyer default. These may include foreclosure, property repossession, or negotiation for a modified agreement.

- **Legal Counsel:** In the event of a dispute, consult with an attorney to explore legal options and ensure your interests are protected.

5. Regulatory Compliance:

- **Local Regulations:** Ensure compliance with all local and state regulations governing seller financing to avoid legal complications or disputes.

6. Diversify Investments:

- **Diversification:** Avoid becoming overly reliant on one seller financing transaction by diversifying your real estate investments.

- **Liquidity Planning:** Plan for potential liquidity challenges by considering how the seller financing agreement will affect your financial stability.

Conclusion

Seller financing can be a powerful tool in real estate transactions, but it's essential for both buyers and sellers to recognize and mitigate the associated risks. By conducting due diligence, seeking professional guidance, negotiating favorable terms, building good relationships, and preparing for default scenarios, both parties can navigate seller financing with confidence.

Ultimately, successful seller financing transactions require a combination of careful planning, clear communication, legal protection, and financial preparedness. When executed prudently, seller financing can be a mutually beneficial arrangement that allows buyers to achieve their homeownership dreams and sellers to achieve their financial goals while minimizing risks for both parties involved.

Chapter 9

Tax Implications and Considerations in Seller Financing

Seller financing in real estate can have significant tax implications for both buyers and sellers. Understanding these implications is crucial to making informed decisions and optimizing the financial benefits of seller financing. In this chapter, we will explore the tax considerations and implications associated with seller financing, providing guidance on how to navigate this complex aspect of real estate transactions.

Tax Considerations for Buyers

Buyers engaging in seller financing should be aware of the following tax considerations:

1. Mortgage Interest Deduction:

Benefit: Buyers may be eligible for a mortgage interest deduction on their federal income taxes. Interest payments made to the seller can often be deducted, reducing the buyer's taxable income.

Limitations: To qualify for this deduction, buyers must meet specific criteria, including itemizing deductions on their tax returns and using the seller financing for the purchase of a qualified residence (typically their primary residence).

2. Capital Gains Treatment:

Benefit: In some cases, seller financing may provide buyers with favorable capital gains treatment. If the seller's financing agreement results in an installment sale, buyers can potentially spread out their capital gains tax liability over the life of the loan.

Eligibility: Buyers must meet certain criteria to qualify for installment sale treatment. Typically, this treatment is available when at least one payment is received in a tax year following the year of the sale.

3. Property Tax Deductions:

Benefit: Property tax payments made by the buyer may also be deductible on their federal income taxes. Buyers should keep records of these payments and consult with a tax professional to maximize their deductions.

Limitations: Deductibility of property taxes may be subject to changes in tax laws, so it's essential to stay informed about current tax regulations.

4. Depreciation Deductions (Investment Properties):

Benefit: Buyers of investment properties financed through seller financing may be eligible to claim depreciation deductions. Depreciation allows investors to deduct a portion of the property's cost each year as an expense, reducing taxable income.

Requirements: To claim depreciation deductions, buyers must adhere to IRS guidelines and have a qualified investment property. Consultation with a tax professional is recommended to ensure compliance.

Tax Considerations for Sellers

Sellers participating in seller financing should also be mindful of various tax considerations:

1. Capital Gains Tax:

Implication: Sellers may be subject to capital gains tax on the profit from the sale of the property. The capital gains tax rate depends on factors such as the seller's income, the length of time they owned the property, and changes in tax laws.

Exclusion: Under certain conditions, sellers may qualify for a capital gains tax exclusion. For example, if the property served as the seller's primary residence for at least two out of the past five years, they may be eligible for a significant exclusion.

2. Interest Income:

Implication: Sellers receive interest income from the buyer's monthly payments. This interest income is generally taxable and should be reported on the seller's income tax return.

Tax Rate: The tax rate applied to interest income depends on the seller's overall income and tax bracket. It may be subject to federal, state, and local taxes.

3. Depreciation Recapture (Investment Properties):

Implication: If the property sold through seller financing is an investment property that the seller previously claimed depreciation on, they may be subject to depreciation recapture upon sale.

Recapture Tax: Depreciation recapture requires sellers to pay taxes on the amount of depreciation they previously deducted. This tax is typically assessed at a higher rate than capital gains tax.

4. Installment Sale Reporting:

Implication: In cases where the seller financing agreement qualifies as an installment sale, sellers can report the sale income and recognize capital gains over the life of the loan.

Advantages: This method can help sellers spread out their tax liability and potentially lower their overall tax rate on the sale income.

5. State and Local Taxes:

Implication: Sellers may be subject to state and local taxes on the sale of real property. Tax rates and regulations vary by location, so sellers should consult with tax professionals familiar with local tax laws.

6. Consultation with Tax Professionals:

Given the complexity of tax regulations and the unique circumstances of each seller financing transaction, it is advisable for both buyers and sellers to consult with tax professionals. These professionals can provide personalized guidance, help navigate the intricacies of tax laws, and ensure compliance with relevant regulations.

Structuring Seller Financing for Tax Efficiency

Buyers and sellers can work together to structure their seller financing agreement in a way that optimizes tax efficiency. Here are some considerations:

1. Capital Gains Spreading:

Buyers and sellers can explore installment sale agreements to spread the capital gains tax liability over several years. This approach can help sellers reduce their overall tax rate and provide buyers with more manageable tax payments.

2. Interest Rate Negotiation:

Buyers can negotiate the interest rate with sellers to ensure that it aligns with their financial goals while still allowing sellers to earn competitive interest income. Finding a balance between an attractive interest rate for buyers and a favorable return for sellers can be mutually beneficial.

3. Structured Payments:

Buyers and sellers can structure the payment schedule to align with their respective financial situations and tax planning. This may involve adjusting the frequency and timing of payments to optimize tax benefits.

4. Compliance with Tax Regulations:

Both parties should ensure that their seller financing agreement complies with all relevant federal, state, and local tax regulations. This includes adhering to IRS guidelines for installment sales and accurately reporting interest income.

5. Consultation with Tax Professionals:

Seeking advice from tax professionals with expertise in real estate transactions is essential. These professionals can provide guidance on tax planning, deductions, and compliance with tax laws, ensuring that both buyers and sellers make informed decisions.

Staying Informed and Adapting

Tax laws and regulations are subject to change, making it essential for both buyers and sellers to stay informed about updates that may affect their seller financing transactions. Tax professionals can assist in monitoring changes and adapting strategies to optimize tax efficiency accordingly.

Conclusion

Seller financing in real estate offers various tax implications and considerations for both buyers and sellers. Understanding these tax implications and structuring seller financing agreements with tax efficiency in mind can lead to mutually beneficial outcomes for both parties. However, due to the complexity of tax laws and the unique nature of each transaction, consultation with tax professionals is highly recommended to ensure compliance and maximize tax benefits.

By taking a proactive approach to tax planning and maintaining compliance with tax regulations, buyers and sellers can navigate the tax aspects of seller financing with confidence, ultimately enhancing the overall success of their real estate transactions.

Chapter 10

Exiting a Seller Financing Agreement

Seller financing agreements in real estate are often long-term commitments that span several years. However, circumstances can change for both buyers and sellers, leading them to consider exiting or modifying the existing agreement. In this chapter, we will explore the various scenarios and strategies for exiting a seller financing agreement, whether it's due to changes in financial situations, property needs, or other factors.

Evaluating the Need for an Exit

Exiting a seller financing agreement is a significant decision that should be made carefully. Before proceeding, both buyers and sellers should assess their motivations and reasons for considering an exit. Here are some common situations that may warrant an exit strategy:

For Buyers:

1. **Financial Hardship:** Buyers may face unforeseen financial challenges, such as job loss, medical expenses, or changes in income, making it difficult to meet their payment obligations.

2. **Changing Housing Needs:** If buyers' housing needs change due to family size, job relocation, or other reasons, they may need to sell the property and exit the agreement.

3. **Refinancing Opportunities:** Buyers may want to explore refinancing options to secure a lower interest rate or more favorable loan terms.

4. **Property Issues:** Unforeseen property issues or damage can make it impractical or costly for buyers to continue owning the property.

For Sellers:

1. **Financial Needs:** Sellers may require immediate access to the remaining balance of the loan for personal financial reasons.

2. **Changes in Investment Goals:** Sellers' investment strategies or goals may evolve, leading them to consider selling the property or modifying the financing agreement.

3. **Buyer Default:** In cases where buyers default on the agreement, sellers may need to exit the agreement to regain ownership of the property and potentially sell it to another buyer.

Exiting Strategies for Buyers

Buyers looking to exit a seller financing agreement should explore the following strategies:

1. Refinancing:

Refinancing involves securing a new mortgage or financing arrangement with more favorable terms. Buyers can approach traditional lenders or private lenders to explore refinancing options.

Considerations:

- Check creditworthiness and financial stability to qualify for refinancing.

- Compare interest rates, loan terms, and fees to ensure a better deal than the existing seller financing agreement.

- Notify the seller of the intent to refinance and coordinate the transition smoothly.

2. Sale of the Property:

Selling the property allows buyers to exit the seller financing agreement while potentially realizing a profit from the sale. Buyers can list the property on the market and find a new buyer.

Considerations:

- Engage a real estate agent to help with the property sale.

- Communicate with the seller regarding the decision to sell and coordinate the sale process.

- Ensure that the sale price covers the remaining balance owed to the seller.

3. Loan Assumption:

In some cases, buyers may find another party willing to assume their seller financing agreement. This means that a new buyer takes over the existing financing terms and continues making payments to the seller.

Considerations:

- Check the terms of the seller financing agreement to see if loan assumption is allowed.

- Obtain approval from the seller and ensure that the new buyer meets the financial requirements.

- Facilitate a smooth transition between the existing and new buyers.

4. Negotiate with the Seller:

Buyers can discuss their financial challenges or reasons for wanting to exit the agreement with the seller. In some cases, sellers may be willing to modify the terms or provide temporary relief to accommodate the buyer's situation.

Considerations:

- Be transparent and open about the reasons for wanting to modify or exit the agreement.

- Negotiate in good faith and explore potential solutions that benefit both parties.

Exiting Strategies for Sellers

Sellers looking to exit a seller financing agreement should consider the following strategies:

1. Negotiate with the Buyer:

Engage in open and honest communication with the buyer to explore possible solutions that address both parties' needs. This may involve modifying the terms of the agreement, extending the loan duration, or allowing the buyer more time to fulfill their obligations.

Considerations:

- Understand the buyer's reasons for seeking modifications or an exit.

- Explore alternative solutions that may align with both parties' goals.

- Consult with legal and financial professionals to ensure any modifications comply with applicable laws.

2. Foreclosure:

In cases where the buyer defaults on the seller financing agreement and cannot resolve the issue, sellers may consider initiating foreclosure proceedings. This process allows sellers to regain ownership of the property.

Considerations:

- Consult with an attorney experienced in real estate and foreclosure laws to navigate the process correctly.

- Ensure compliance with local and state foreclosure regulations.

- Be prepared for potential legal costs and lengthy proceedings.

3. Sell the Note:

Sellers can opt to sell the seller financing note to investors or financial institutions. Selling the note provides sellers with a lump sum of cash, transferring the responsibility for collecting payments to the note buyer.

Considerations:

- Research potential buyers of seller financing notes and obtain competitive offers.

- Be aware that selling the note may result in a lower sale price than the original property value.

- Ensure legal and financial due diligence when transferring the note.

4. Lease-Option Agreements:

Sellers can consider entering into lease-option agreements with the buyers. In this scenario, the buyer leases the property with an option to purchase it at a later date, giving both parties more flexibility.

Considerations:

- Draft a clear lease-option agreement that outlines the terms, including the purchase price and option period.

- Ensure compliance with local landlord-tenant laws when entering into such agreements.

- Determine whether a portion of the lease payments will be credited toward the purchase price.

Legal and Financial Considerations

Exiting a seller financing agreement involves legal and financial complexities that vary based on the specific circumstances and the terms of the original agreement. Both buyers and sellers should consider the following legal and financial considerations:

Legal Consultation:

Engage legal professionals, such as real estate attorneys, to provide guidance on the exit strategy chosen. Attorneys can help ensure that all legal requirements are met and that the exit process is executed correctly.

Tax Implications:

Exiting a seller financing agreement may have tax implications for both buyers and sellers. Consult with tax professionals to understand the tax consequences of the chosen exit strategy and to plan accordingly.

Documentation:

Proper documentation is essential when exiting a seller financing agreement. Ensure that all agreements, modifications, and transactions are well-documented to protect both parties' interests.

Conclusion

Exiting a seller financing agreement in real estate requires careful consideration, open communication, and adherence to legal and financial best practices. Whether it's due to changing financial circumstances, property needs, or other factors, buyers and sellers have several strategies at their disposal to navigate the exit process effectively. It is essential to seek professional guidance, engage in transparent communication, and approach the exit with a clear understanding of the implications and responsibilities involved.

By approaching the exit process thoughtfully and responsibly, both parties can achieve a resolution that aligns with their goals and circumstances, ultimately ensuring a successful transition out of the seller financing agreement.

Bonus Chapter

Building Strong Seller Relationships for Favorable Seller Financing Deals

In the world of real estate, establishing and nurturing strong relationships with sellers can be the key to securing favorable seller financing deals. While the financial terms of a transaction are crucial, the human element — the trust, understanding, and rapport between buyer and seller — can often be the decisive factor. In this bonus chapter, we will explore why building a relationship with a seller is the best way to get a favorable seller financing deal and offer valuable tips on how to foster these connections.

The Power of Relationships in Real Estate

Seller financing is not just a financial transaction; it's a partnership. Both buyers and sellers have their own motivations, goals, and concerns. Building a strong relationship helps bridge the gap between these interests and creates an atmosphere of mutual respect and cooperation. Here's why relationships matter:

1. Trust and Confidence

Trust is the foundation of any successful seller financing deal. Sellers need to have confidence that buyers will fulfill their obligations, make timely payments, and take care of the property. Buyers, on the other hand, need assurance that sellers will uphold their end of the agreement and provide support when needed.

2. Flexibility in Negotiations

A strong seller-buyer relationship often leads to more flexible and accommodating negotiations. When both parties trust each other's intentions, they are more likely to explore creative solutions that benefit everyone. This can result in better terms, lower interest rates, and a smoother transaction.

3. Understanding and Empathy

Real estate transactions can be complex, and unforeseen challenges may arise. A strong seller-buyer relationship fosters understanding and empathy between the parties. Sellers may be more willing to accommodate buyers facing temporary financial difficulties, and buyers may be understanding of unexpected issues on the seller's side.

4. Easier Problem-Solving

In the event of disputes or unexpected hurdles, a positive relationship provides a foundation for effective problem-solving. Both parties are more likely to work together to find mutually beneficial solutions rather than resorting to legal action or contentious negotiations.

Tips for Building Strong Seller Relationships

Building a strong relationship with a seller takes time, effort, and genuine interest in their needs and concerns. Here are some tips to help you foster these crucial connections:

1. Open and Honest Communication

Establish a foundation of open and honest communication from the beginning. Discuss your goals, motivations, and concerns transparently. This sets the tone for a trusting and cooperative relationship.

2. Active Listening

Listen attentively to the seller's perspective. Understand their reasons for offering seller financing and their expectations for the transaction. Show empathy and respect for their point of view.

3. Personalize Your Approach

Recognize that every seller is unique. Tailor your approach to each seller's personality and preferences. Some may prefer formal discussions, while others may appreciate a more informal and friendly interaction.

4. Demonstrated Reliability

Consistently demonstrate your reliability by fulfilling your commitments and meeting deadlines. Show that you are a responsible and trustworthy buyer who takes the seller's interests seriously.

5. Share Your Vision

Clearly communicate your vision for the property and how seller financing aligns with your long-term goals. Sellers are more likely to support buyers who have a well-defined plan for the property.

6. Be Patient and Respectful

Realize that building a strong relationship may take time. Be patient and respectful, especially if the seller is hesitant or cautious. Avoid applying undue pressure, as it can strain the relationship.

7. Address Concerns Proactively

If the seller has concerns or questions, address them promptly and professionally. Provide information and documentation to alleviate any doubts or uncertainties.

8. Regular Updates

Keep the seller informed about the progress of the transaction. Regular updates create a sense of involvement and reduce anxiety on the seller's part.

9. Show Appreciation

Express gratitude and appreciation for the seller's willingness to consider seller financing. Small gestures of thanks can go a long way in strengthening the relationship.

10. Stay Connected

Maintain contact with the seller even after the transaction is complete. A lasting relationship can lead to future opportunities, referrals, and a network of valuable connections in the real estate market.

Real-Life Success Stories

To illustrate the power of building strong seller relationships, here are a few real-life success stories:

Story 1: The Reluctant Seller

A seller was initially hesitant about offering seller financing due to past negative experiences. The buyer took the time to build trust by addressing the seller's concerns, sharing their vision for the property, and staying in touch regularly. As a result, the seller agreed to seller financing with favorable terms, and both parties enjoyed a smooth and successful transaction.

Story 2: The Flexible Negotiation

In a challenging market, a seller faced difficulties finding a buyer willing to offer favorable terms. The buyer approached the seller with empathy and a willingness to work together. Through open communication and flexibility in negotiations, they crafted an agreement that benefited both parties and led to a successful transaction.

Conclusion

In the world of seller financing in real estate, building strong relationships with sellers is not just a bonus—it's often the key to securing favorable terms and a successful transaction. Trust, transparency, and cooperation are the cornerstones of these relationships, and they can lead to flexible negotiations, creative solutions, and a more enjoyable experience for both buyers and sellers.

Remember that each seller is unique, so adapt your approach to fit their individual needs and preferences. By investing time and effort into building strong seller relationships, you can maximize the benefits of seller financing and create lasting connections in the real estate market.